Benny and Toby Stay Safe at Home

Father said to Benny, "Son, we are going out. We will be back soon. Be good and stay safe." Benny replied "ok Father. Bye."

Benny's friend, Toby, was also there with him. Mother said, "I have kept lemonade for both of you enjoy" Soon, the parents left the house.

Now, Benny was a good boy but Toby was very naughty. He asked, "Benny, what do we do now?" Benny replied, "Let us drink the lemonade first."

So, they started drinking the lemonade. Toby, while drinking, dropped some on the floor. Benny quickly brought a mop and swept the floor.

Toby cried, "What are you doing? Leave it." Benny said, "No. Someone might slip on it. It could even be you." Toby cried, "Oh! I did not think about that."

But Toby was restless. He said, "Let us play with your toys." So, they started playing with the toys. Soon, both got bored. Benny started picking up his toys.

Toby said, "Leave them. Let us eat something." Benny said, "I always keep my toys back after playing. Someone can trip over them and get hurt."

While coming down stairs, Toby said, "Benny let us race down the stairs." Benny cried, "What? Are you mad? Either of us can fall and hurt ourselves. No way."

Toby said, "You are right." Soon, both were in the kitchen. Toby saw a knife and picked it. Immediately, Benny took it from him and kept it back.

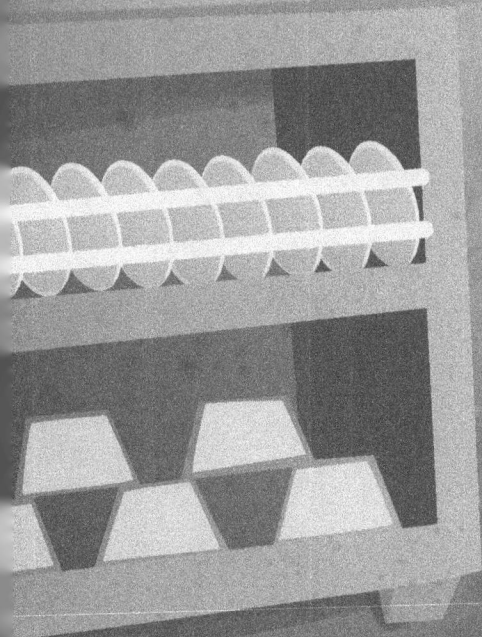

But Toby was not going to give up easily. He saw a box of matches. He quickly picked the box and took out a matchstick. Before Benny could stop him, he hurriedly lit a match but hurt himself instead. "Ouch!" he cried. And the matchstick fell on the floor.

Benny picked the matchstick and threw it in the dustbin. Then, he said to Toby, "See, you got hurt."

They took apples from the fruit basket and started eating them. After eating the apples, they washed their hands.

Toby said, "My favourite cartoon show is coming on the television. Let us watch it." As he was about to switch on the television, Benny stopped him.

He said, "You just washed your hands. They are wet. Do not touch the electric switch with wet hands. You might get a shock."

"Oh!" cried Toby. So, he wiped his hands with a dry cloth first. Then, he switched on the television. As they were watching the cartoon, the phone rang.

Benny picked up the phone. It was for his father. He said, "My father cannot come to the phone right now. Can I have him call you back?"

After keeping the phone down, Toby asked, "But your father is out? Why did you lie?" Benny replied, "We are alone here. It is not safe to tell anyone that my parents are out."

Toby said, "Smart boy." Suddenly, the bell rang. Toby ran to open it but Benny stopped him. He told Toby to be quiet. The bell rang again. And then, after a while, there was silence.

Benny said, "We should not open the door when we are alone at home. Who knows who is outside?" Toby said, "True."

When Benny's parents came back, Benny told them everything. Mother praised, "Well! Our little boys have become experts on being safe."

Glossary

Safe: free from harm

lemonade: a drink made with the juice of lemons, water and sugar

naughty: behave badly

swept: to clean

slip: fall over

restless: unable to rest

bored: feeling unhappy because something is not interesting

trip: fall

no way: no

hurriedly: quickly

lit: burnt

expert: a person with a high level of knowledge